Woodstock Handmade Houses

Robert Haney and David Ballantine
Jonathan Elliott, photographer

Dedicated to all our owner-builders, for
their wonderful hospitality, and to everyone
who helped us find them. And, to all the
other great houses we just couldn't
include—our apologies.

ISBN 0-345-25592-5-695

Manufactured in the United States of America

First Edition: October 1974
Third Printing: June 1976

Woodstock Handmade Houses/Preface

When the American dream still seemed a good trip, about seventy years ago, some nonconformists got together to explore a different lifestyle up in Woodstock, where the Catskill mountains start getting tall. They were mostly artists, craftsmen, tinkerers, and thinkers. In those days they got labeled: Bohemians. Today, perhaps they'd be tagged freaks. Their first shelters were sometimes just a hunk of oilcloth or a free flop in a farmer's barn. But when they really started to build they went heavy on imagination, light on money.

Up the local creeks, water-turned saws changed "big sticks" into cheap boards, and bluestone quarry rubble was free. A lot of those original studios, shacks, huts and hovels are still keeping the warmth in and the snow out in this four-season environment. A few of the original owner-builders are still around, still faithful to their different dream. They've fired the fantasies of three generations since, and sometimes the same hammers they used now bang in younger hands, putting together everything from plain hutches to pretty wild wickiups.

So doing it yourself is nothing new in Woodstock. What's more, in any of the older handmade houses you can still share in the lives of those first inspired hammerers. You can get closer yet by just hewing a beam and slamming it into place yourself. That's the deepest you'll ever get into any structure.

Thus, "Woodstock" became a word people used when they talked about imagination and self-sufficiency and getting together with your environment. It still means that today, and to a lot more people.
Take Clarence's place.

His house is gone now. But until a few years back it was an ongoing process, a vision that went beyond four walls and a roof. Parts of it would be dying while others were being born. And when Clarence had to quit scrounging the Chevy hubcaps and other junk essential to his dream, the place totally died. But not before a flock of younger pilgrims found him out and started building to his message: Don't look to find yourself in other people's trips, and with imagination you can make a new natural resource out of what other people throw away.

The authors have built their own homes too, but these are not included here—we found too many other imaginative shelters we thought you'd like to see. One of us grew up in a homemade house and started his own next door. For years it was just a garage-like thing, the upstairs a litter of tools, the downstairs shared by an old Mack truck and a Hispano-Suiza touring car. During a protracted bachelorhood progress was slow. The surge came with marriage to a woman with three children. Working by lantern, then electric light and lots of weekends on a ladder, brought us all inside. We've settled in, but a deck out toward the mountain's face sure would be nice, and someday a bedroom of the grownups' own. The planning never stops—the building pauses—maybe not tomorrow—but once you've got your start it's easy to carry on.

The other of us fell heir to a falling-down barn by the local slaughter-house. After a summer of toil and learning respect for how tight those old farmers built, it metamorphosed into his own private refuge. A left-handed carpenter and flycaster, he's also a writer, and it was good therapy between nerve-jangling trips to New York City to take it all out on defenseless nails and chestnut pins. He doesn't exactly recommend thirty straight ten-hour days, but it does get a place finally finished.

Anyway, we both agree...the more builders, the less bombers.

In making this book we drove up many dead-end, washed-out roads and hiked farther on when they pinched out in places where "contractor" is a discouraging word. We met happy people, got embraced by their hospitality, and marveled at the many different ways they had found to keep the rain off their stained-glass making, pottery wheels, looms, and bread baking. Some of the best shelters started life as something else: barns, schoolhouses, even churches. (The pews were gone—but then living well is a religion good as any.) Often, you had to look twice to recognize the materials they used—but they worked, and with luck they were free.

In some of these houses the owners have decided to live without electricity and adopt some old wood stove, which makes rate-hikes other people's problem. But the important thing was how these old places were salvaged from abandonment and lack of love. That's a real ecology—revering materials and the long-ago labor of other self-builders. Really look, and you can still see what those old-timers wrote with an adze on the side of a beam.

Every shelter pictured here was once a dream. If this book helps you to get your house out of your head and onto the ground, or just raise one wall, or even see through an old window differently, then it's a job well done. All it takes is getting started and enough friends to help you keep going. Local sawmills continue to turn out cheap rough boards, and old quarries, dumps, and junkyards remain to be picked over. Later, it'll be a hassle for the tax assessor to figure the true value of your handiwork, but the first time you sit down and look around at it, you'll know!

ROBERT HANEY
DAVID BALLANTINE
Woodstock, New York
June, 1974

Chicken wire was stretched over a network of woven saplings.
Then for one long day forty people mixed and troweled until there was a home.

If you luck into a nearby Ashram that peddles great salvage, you'd buy this window for two hundred dollars, like the young couple who now have an archangel sharing their resurrected barn.

A fine new house and another young couple heavily into stained glass, ceramics and quilting with home-dyed swatches. They have no secrets from their plants.

Long on the land, a sculptor muscled out the
bluestone for his house, healed the quarry hole
with spring water, and had himself a swimming
pool. The fish handle the maintenance.

These tiles have never been in a store.
The tile maker's kiln is just beyond her kitchen door.

The view from the throne…

…and a see-through Buddha.

An astrologer high on a mountainside always knows where her stars are.

The home dome in a sculptor's personal Shangri-la

A sanctuary for the human imagination.
If it happens to embrace the karma of an ancient oak,
all the better.

...and above this level there is only sky.

The granddaddy of all the hippies got himself into a lot of paintings.
Hervey built a whole colony, scattering rough cabins like seeds. When you were broke
he never asked for rent. Of course, you helped him to build...

…his concert hall.

Warmth can be beautiful...

A saved church and the best salvage we ever saw. The fireplace, from the men's room lobby of an old movie palace, was a jigsaw puzzle that didn't fool one of our local masons. But you better believe, it was more than a one-six-pack job.

He built his house and the environment to go with it,
one man's forty-year love affair with stone.

...and quiet neighbors in the backyard pond who never begrudge you a breakfast trout or two.

Surprises, little…

. . . and big. A turning mill turned house. The thirty foot water wheel waits as though it always has known fossil fuels are not forever.

Almost a Navaho hogan, this octagon of interlocked hardwood logs is crowned by a wheel of light. The power company hasn't scribbled on their sky with wires.

The path ends at a new-
raised saphouse, where the
commune makes the
best maple syrup that's
ever tickled our tongues.

You can live in your studio and work in your living room,
if you stash them both under a gullwing roof.

The mountain church of everybody's favorite hippie priest. The party to celebrate
his ninety years was held beside the rectory he raised with his own hands. Small outside,
but within you'll find a cathedral.

Smaller structures.

If you can only scrounge enough slate
and other stuff to make a playhouse for
your child, it'll beat anything you can buy.

Automation retired a railroad guard
and his hut went to pasture in a grimeless garden.

If it's a good place to wake up, it's got to be a good place to sleep…in a one-room home…

…or where Bob Dylan used to.

A smiling foundation seems a good way to start a house.

A yurt for all seasons, with a skin of handsewn canvas and cold-forged conduit for ribs.

A tall girl builds a tall house…

while another hangs free rug
samples for colorful insulation.

A dome perched on a diamond creates lots of thought-starting angles. The owner has done it all, and between banging on shingles, he helps other heads grapple with Tibetan…

...and once somehow the sky got into the house.

Built in 1802, this glass worker's house
was saved from rot and dragged up a mountain
for a fresh start.

The boss, a German baron, had a house
that never got moved. After a succession of
uncaring owners, a painter and his tile-maker wife,
finally liberated the classic design that lay cringing
under layers of bad taste.

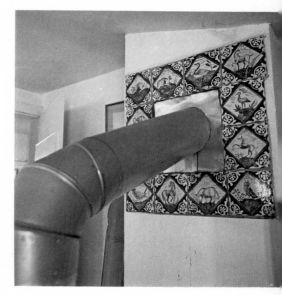

The furniture he makes is his art, and around it this craftsman built a sun-loving house.

A great kitchen, and the cook paints on the furniture.

One day we managed to get lost and this bark-on, cob-rough cabin kind of ambushed us. No palace, but some dude knew enough to use autumn leaves for insulation.

Here, we've always known that buses can be for sleeping.

If all the good barns are already taken, there's nothing to stop you from building your own.

All authentic materials, and still a-building. Native stone and wood, and copper flashed throughout.

No union scale here—just lots of good friends doing it like "they" don't anymore.

Bill's place. Years ago he sawed your trees into boards and beams for fifteen dollars a thousand. Now he's old and the mill's a wreck. We went by just to visit and the camera clicked just once from habit. Maybe his house is the most beautiful of all. He built it more than fifty years ago and all he spent was fifty dollars for cement and lime. The land gave him everything else.

The authors, the photographer, and a friend showing a timber where to go. The house finished nicely, too. It took a year for the rough pine stringers to dry. Then the stairs got made—and we got our ladder back.